ISLAMIC DESIGNS
IN COLOR

N. Simakoff

DOVER PUBLICATIONS, INC.
New York

Published in Canada by General Publishing Company, Ltd., 30 Lesmill Road, Don Mills, Toronto, Ontario.

Islamic Designs in Color, first published by Dover Publications, Inc., in 1993, reproduces (in a modified layout and sequence) all the plates from the portfolio *Iskusstvo Sredneĭ Azii . . . / L'art de l'Asie Centrale . . .* [see Publisher's Note for full translation of title], originally published in Saint Petersburg, 1883, by the Imperatorskie Obščestvo Pooščreniya Khudožestv (Imperial Society for the Encouragement of the Fine Arts). The present edition contains a new Publisher's Note and new captions based on the Russian and French texts accompanying the original portfolio.

Manufactured in the United States of America
Dover Publications, Inc., 31 East 2nd Street, Mineola, N.Y. 11501

Library of Congress Cataloging-in-Publication Data

Simakov, N. (Nikolaĭ), d. 1886.
    [Iskusstvo Sredneĭ Azii. English]
    Islamic designs in color / N. Simakoff.
        p.   cm. — (Dover pictorial archive series)
    "Reproduces (in a modified layout and sequence) all the plates from the portfolio Iskusstvo Sredneĭ Azii . . . / L'art de l'Asie Centrale . . . originally published in Saint Petersburg, 1883 by the Imperatorskie Obščestvo Pooščreniya Khudožestv (Imperial Society for the Encouragement of the Fine Arts). The present edition contains a new publisher's note and new captions based on the Russian and French texts accompanying the original portfolio"—Verso t.p.
    ISBN 0-486-27477-2 (pbk.)
    1. Decoration and ornament, Islamic—Uzbekistan. 2. Decoration and ornament—Uzbekistan. 3. Decoration and ornament, Islamic—Turkmenistan. 4. Decoration and ornament—Turkmenistan. 5. Color in design.
I. Title. II. Series.
NK1475.7.U9S5613   1993
745.4'49584—dc20
                                                         92-32888
                                                              CIP

PUBLISHER'S NOTE

The Islamic works of art illustrated in this book are all from Central Asia, chiefly from the Uzbek and Turkmen Republics of the former Soviet Union. The people of this area are generally of Turkic, Iranian and Mongol stock, and not Arabs, but have progressively accepted Islam ever since the first Arab conquests in the region in the eighth century A.D. Over the millennia this vast area has often been divided into numerous shifting petty states, but has also often been under unified rule—for instance, under the Mongols; under the great Central Asian conqueror Tamerlane (Timur, died 1405); and under the Russians, who expanded into the region in the nineteenth century and had annexed much of it by the 1870s. All twentieth-century tourists who have visited the great architectural and art centers Bukhara and Samarkand in Uzbekistan have done so under Russian auspices.

In 1879 the Russian government sent a scientific expedition to explore its newly acquired Central Asian territory. One member was the art historian N. Simakoff, who copied many monuments and, upon his return, published the portfolio the plates of which are reproduced here. The original text was in Russian and French. A full translation of the typographic Russian title reads: "Art of Central Asia / A Collection of Central Asian Ornament / Rendered from the Originals by / N. Ye. Simakoff. / Awarded a silver medal at the Moscow Art and Industry Exhibition in 1882. / Published by the Imperial Society for the Encouragement of the Fine Arts. / Saint Petersburg. / 1883. / Printed in the cartographic establishment of A. Ilyin." The calligraphic Russian title forming part of Plate 1 reads in translation: "Art of Central Asia. Collection of ornaments and designs rendered from the original architectural monuments and from ceramics, weavings, jewelry and other objects by the member of the Samara* scholarly expedition N. Simakoff in 1879." Each of the individual plates is credited to Simakoff except for Plates 64 and 68, where the artist credit reads "Vil'ye" (Villiers?), and 66, which is credited to the architect A. Kochetoff and dated September 8, 1882.

---

*The members of the expedition assembled in Samara (on the Volga; later called Kuibyshev) before proceeding together into Central Asia.

Simakoff's publication is typical of those chromolithographed portfolios produced all over Europe in the nineteenth century, meant to offer inspiration to craftsmen and commercial artists, and models for manufacturers desirous of upgrading the artistic quality of their products in an increasingly competitive world market. He reproduces designs from carpets and other textiles; tiles; carved wood, plaster and stone; decorative painting on architecture; jewelry and other metalwork; dishes; etc.

The original portfolio contained fifty plates. Wherever an original plate could readily be divided in two, this has been done here in order to offer larger images; there are thus 68 plates in this Dover edition. The captions, although based on those in the original work, are new; they are not only more concise, but have also been brought up to date insofar as possible with regard to place names, names of monuments and location of objects (current standard guidebooks to the former Soviet Union have been consulted).

Following are translations of Russian matter that appears on some additional plates:

Plate 65: "The Gur Emir in Samarkand. Timur's Tomb."

Plate 66: "The Gur Emir in Samarkand. Timur's Tomb. / 1. Display monuments of Tamerlane and his family. 2. Tombs in the vault of Tamerlane and his relatives. 3. Mosque built by Tamerlane's wife. 4. Later constructions. 5. Courtyard in the mosque. 6. Side entrance to the mosque. 7. Main entrance. 8 & 9. Tombs of later descendants of Timur. / General plan of the Gur Emir in Samarkand. Timur's Tomb."

LIST OF PLATES

THE PLATES

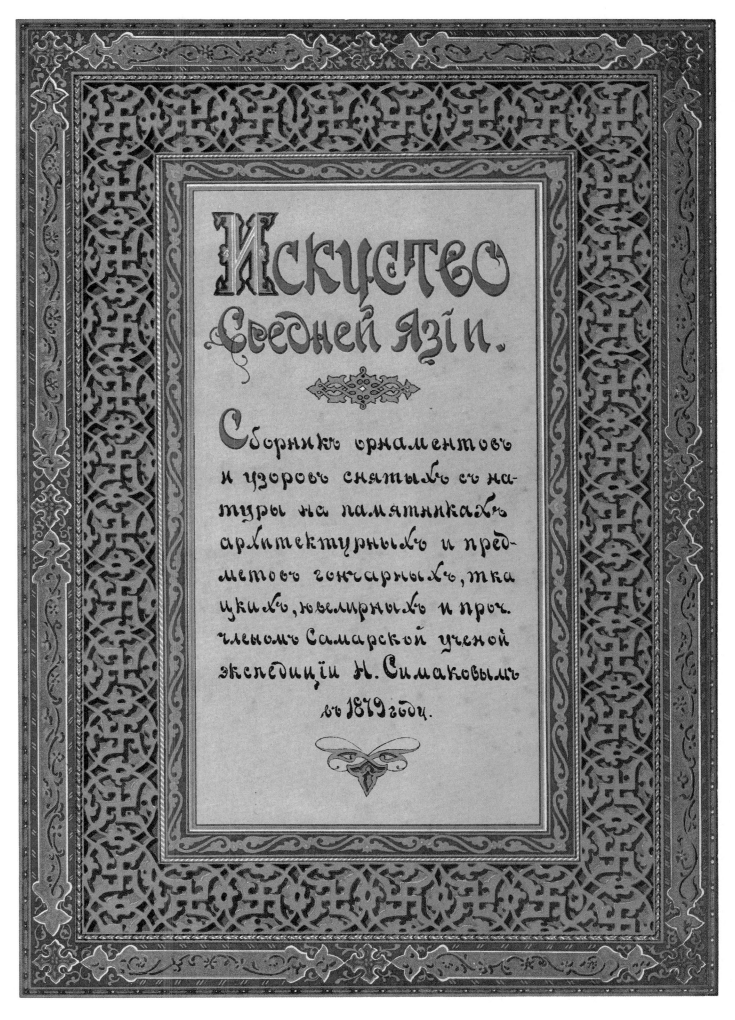

Искуство Средней Азіи.

Сборникъ орнаментовъ и цзоровъ снятыхъ съ натуры на памятникахъ архитектурныхъ и предметовъ гончарныхъ, ткацкихъ, ювелирныхъ и проч. членомъ Самарской ученой экспедиціи Н. Симаковымъ въ 1879 году.

Original title page (translated in Publisher's Note, page v); based on a carved,
gilt and painted wooden coffer cover made in Samarkand.

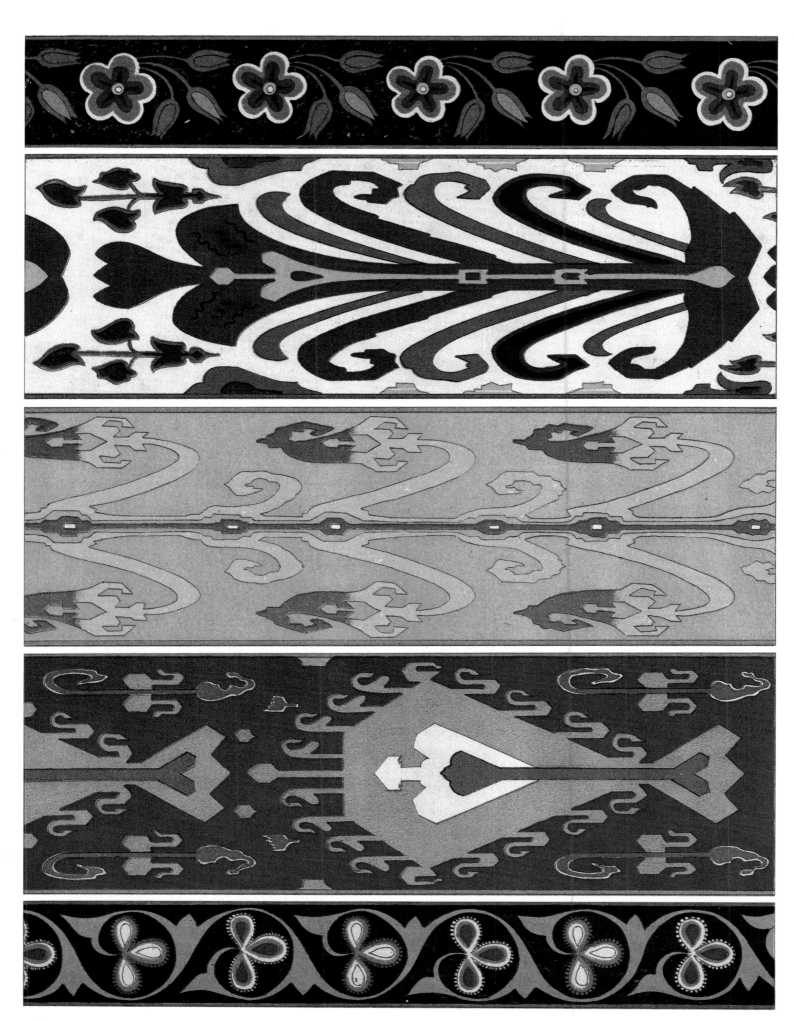

Designs from silk and velvet textiles made in the Bukhara area.

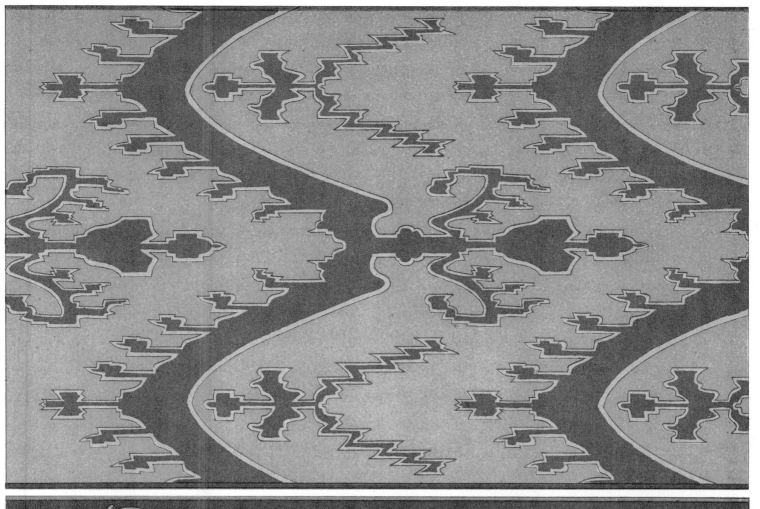

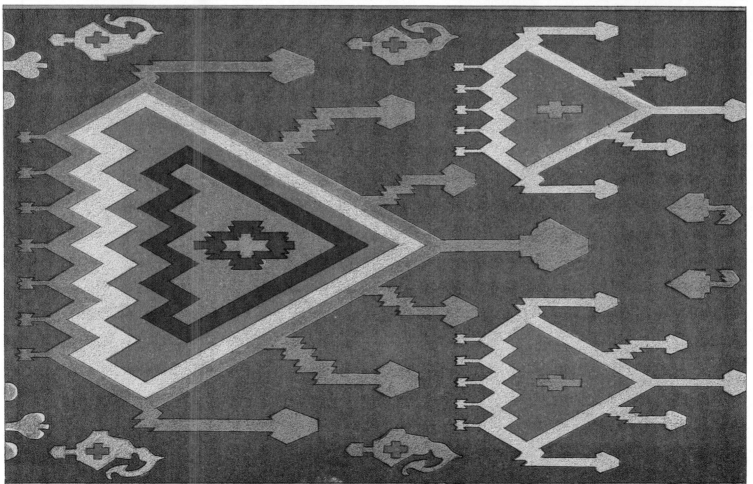

Designs from silk and velvet textiles made in the Bukhara area.

3

Designs from silk and velvet textiles made in the Bukhara area.

Designs from silk and velvet textiles made in the Bukhara area.

Stamped baked-clay bricks from old buildings in Kuldja (now in Xinjiang, China), including two rooftop antefixes (top, left and right).

Designs from carpet friezes in nomadic Turkmen felt tents (heraldic symbols of tribes or families).

Turkmen carpet designs, each associated with a single family.

Turkmen carpet designs.

Part of a carved-wood, ivory-inlaid door from the Khazaret Hodja Yassavi
Mausoleum-Mosque in Turkestan, built by Tamerlane in the years 1397 ff.

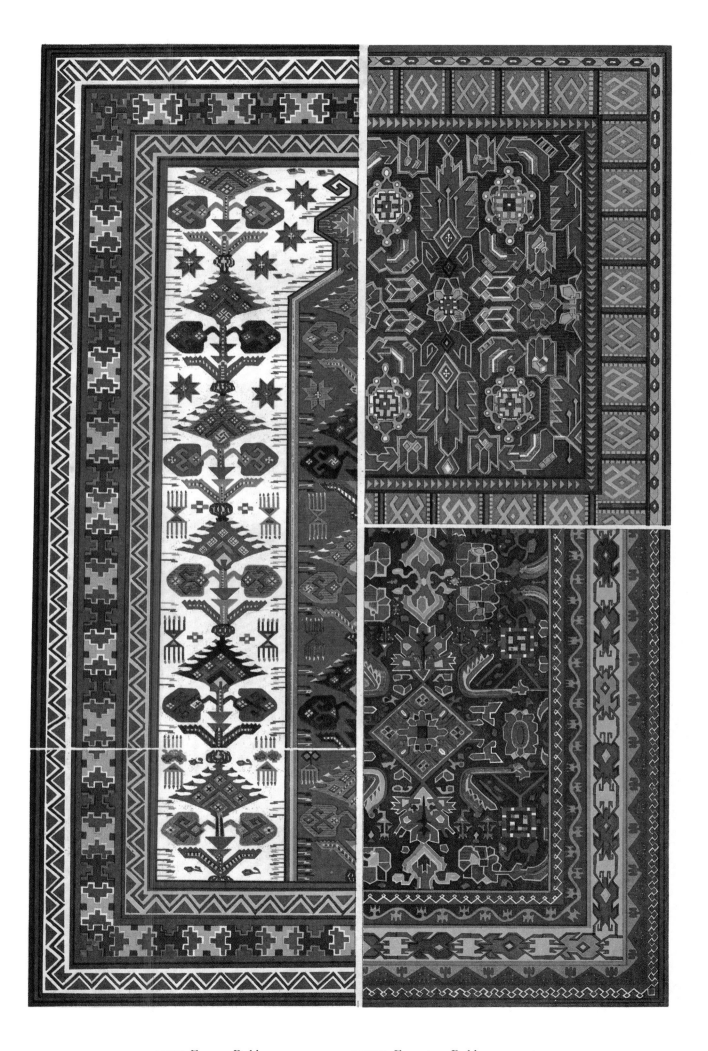

LEFT: From a Bukhara prayer rug. RIGHT: From two Bukhara carpets.

11

LEFT: Turkmen carpet design. RIGHT: Motifs from Turkmen saddle girths and other narrow weavings.

Bukhara carpet design with scorpion and tarantula motifs.

14   Part of a door from a late-15th-century mosque in the Necropolis of Shakhi-
Zinda in Samarkand.

TOP & BOTTOM LEFT: Silk embroideries from robes. BOTTOM RIGHT: Silk and gold embroidery from a leather falconer's gauntlet. All Tadjik (local Iranian) work.

15

Low-relief ornaments from casket covers made in Tashkent.

16

Low-relief ornaments from casket covers made in Tashkent.

17

Design from decorative painting on Bukhara architecture.

Design from decorative painting on Bukhara architecture.

19

Designs from decorative painting on Bukhara architecture.

Designs from decorative painting on Bukhara architecture.

21

Jewelry made by Tadjiks in Tashkent, including an earring, a brooch, a hairpin, prayer cases and bands for head and neck.

Jewelry and other metalwork made by Tadjiks in Tashkent: buckle, dish,
doorpull, earring, knife, sheath, etc.

Teapot of repoussé and engraved tinned copper, made in Kokand.

Designs from decorative painting on Bukhara architecture.

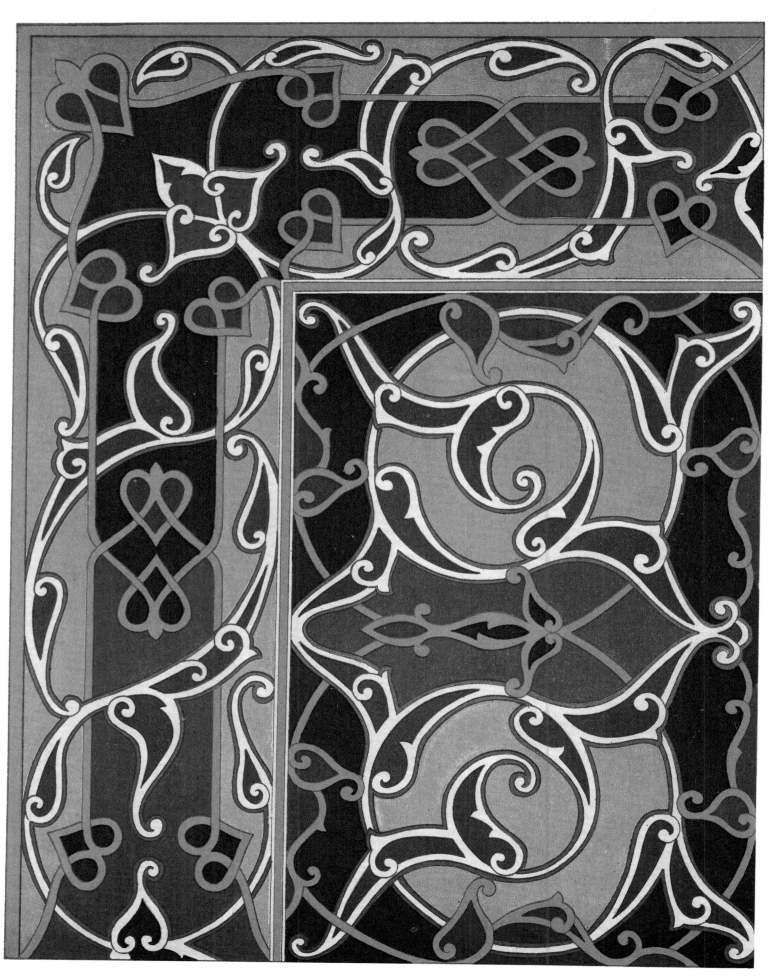

Designs from decorative painting on Bukhara architecture.

Design from decorative painting on Bukhara architecture.

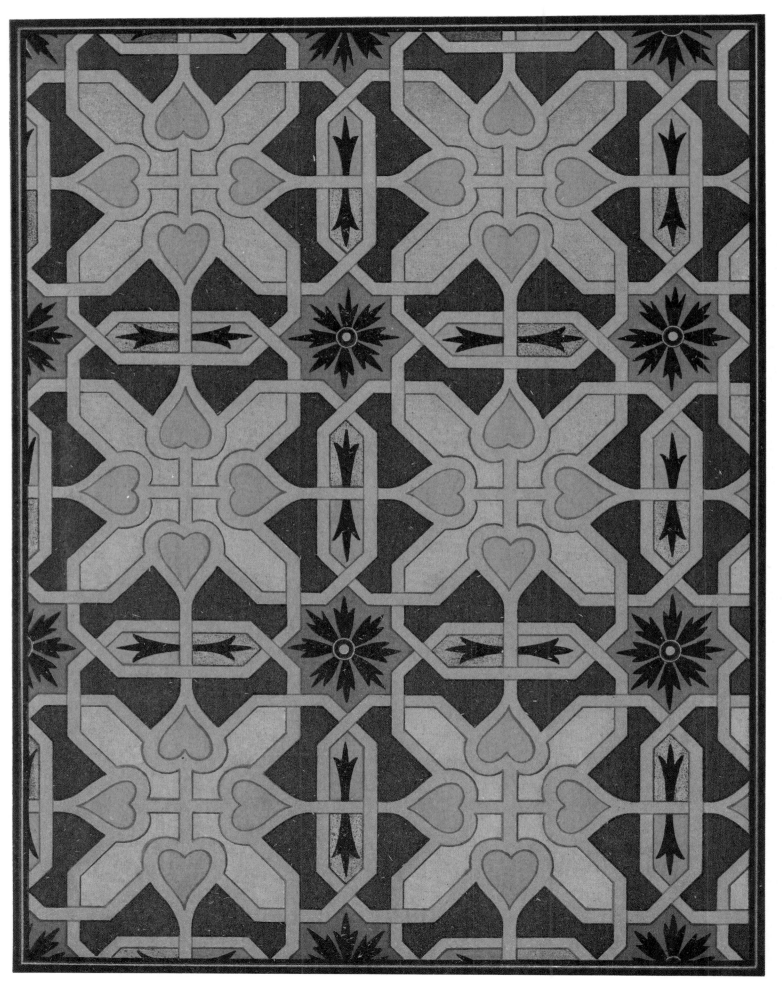

Design from decorative painting on Bukhara architecture.

28

Design from decorative painting on Bukhara architecture.

29

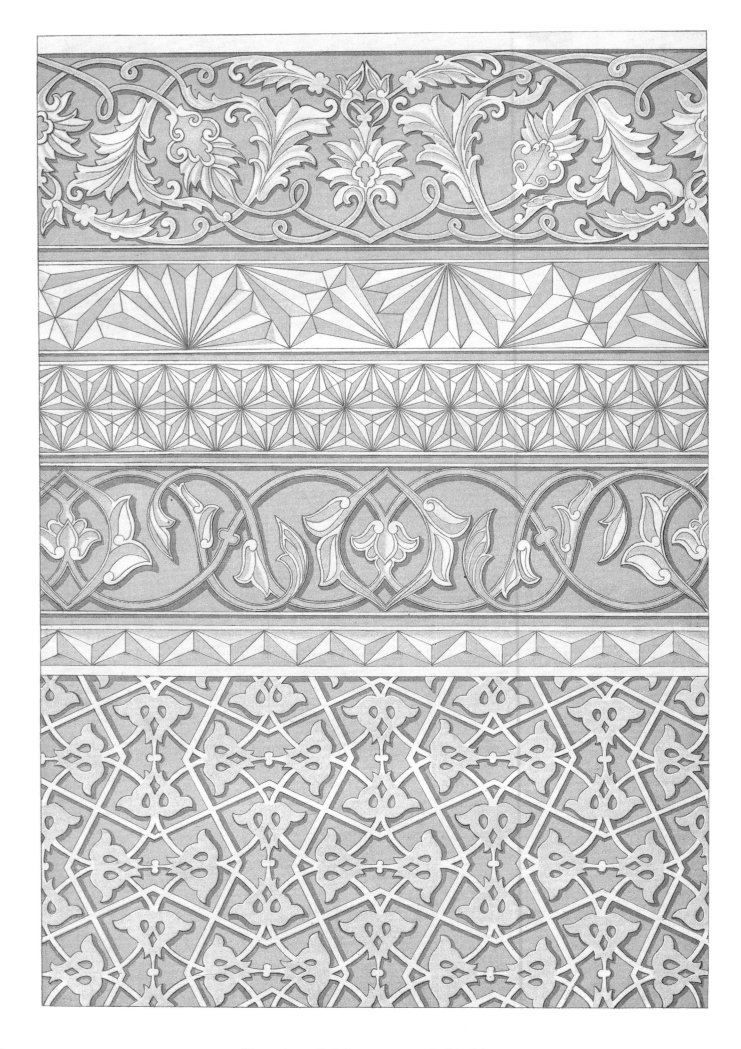

30   Plaster bas-reliefs from a mosque in Khodzhent.

Design from decorative painting on Bukhara architecture.

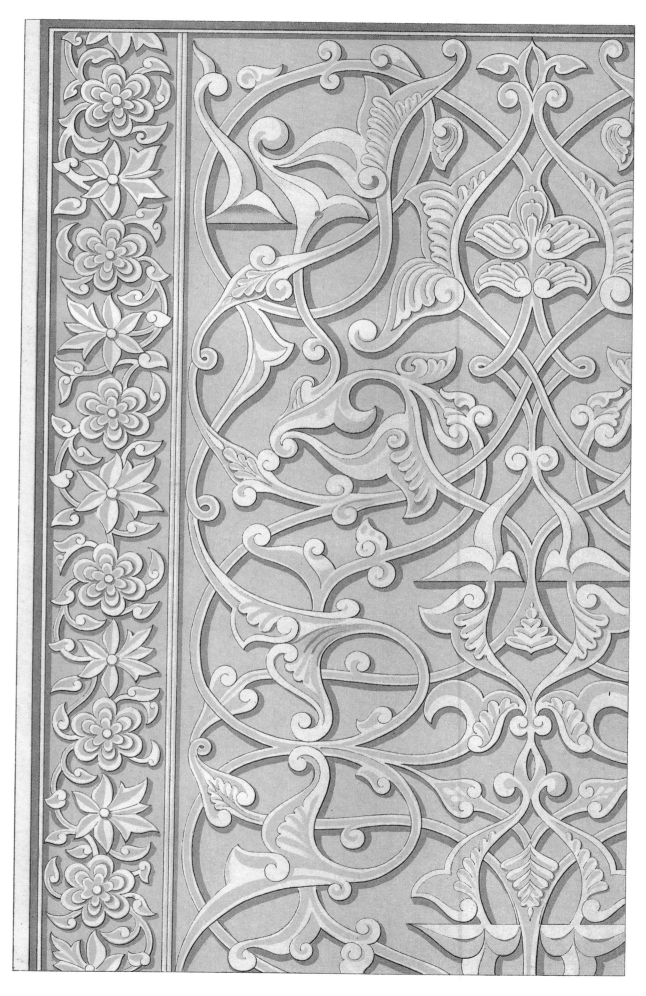

Carved ornament on the sides of the Kok-Tash, the former coronation stone of
the emirs of Bukhara, now in the Gur Emir mausoleum in Samarkand.

Design from decorative painting on Bukhara architecture.

Design from decorative painting on Bukhara architecture.

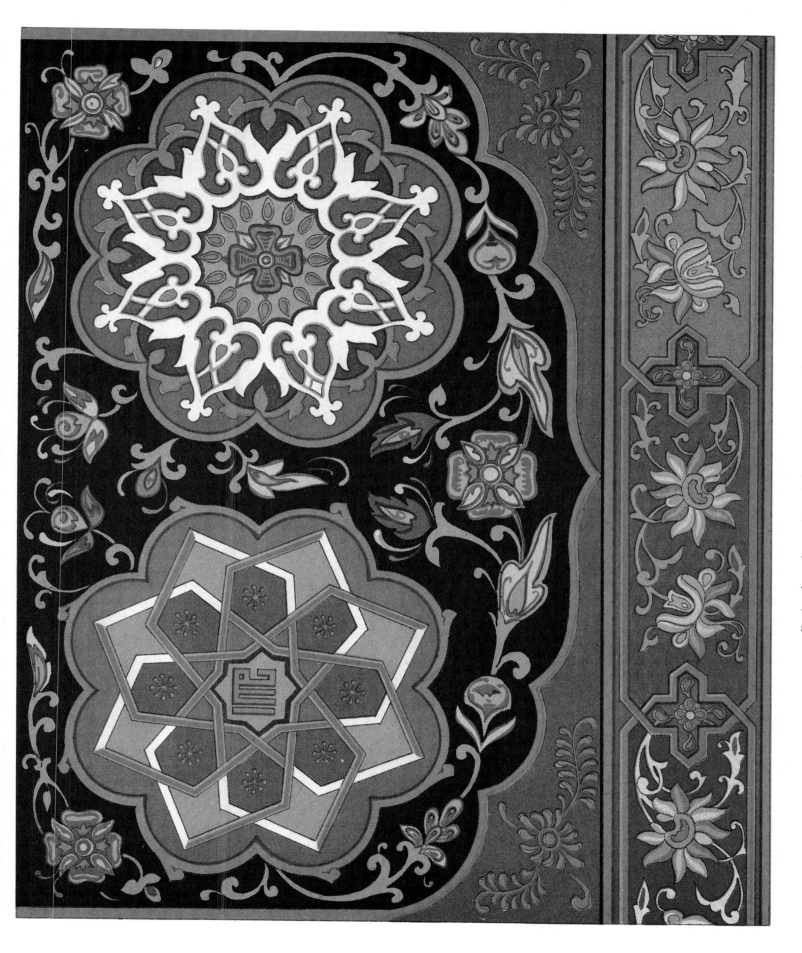

Design from decorative painting on Bukhara architecture.

35

Design from decorative painting on Bukhara architecture.

Design from decorative painting on Bukhara architecture.

37

Design from decorative painting on Bukhara architecture.

Design from decorative painting on Bukhara architecture.

Design from decorative painting on Bukhara architecture.

Design from decorative painting on Bukhara architecture.

41

42

Design from decorative painting on Bukhara architecture.

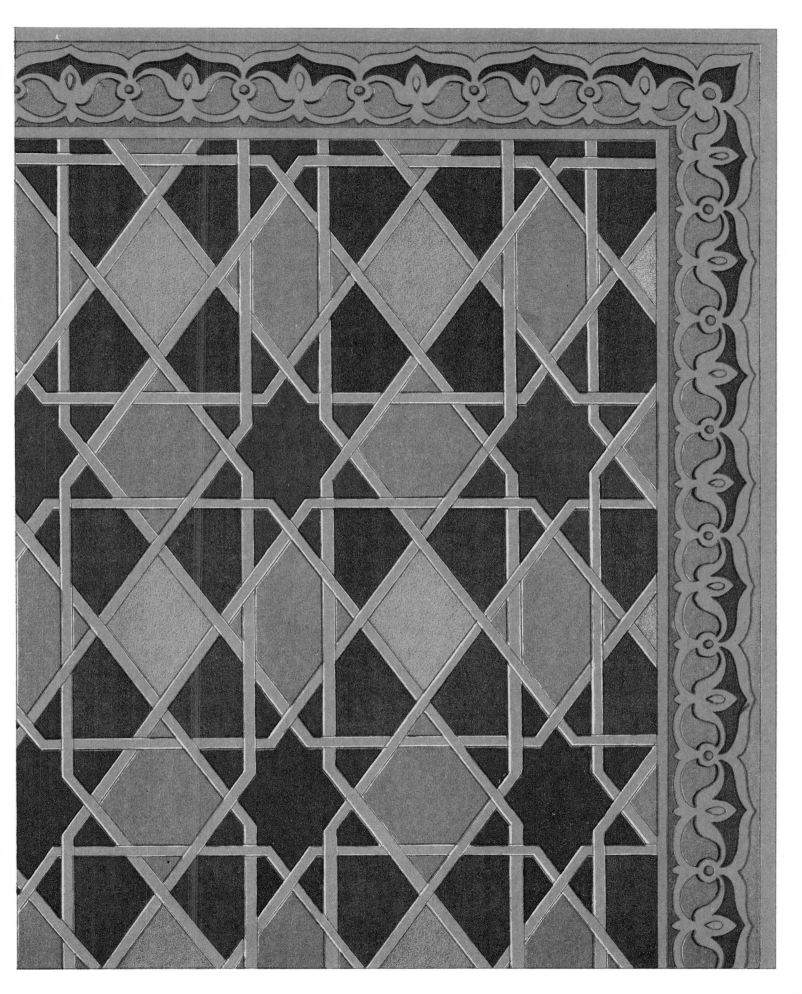

Design from decorative painting on Bukhara architecture.

Design from decorative painting on Bukhara architecture.

Design from decorative painting on Bukhara architecture.

45

TOP TWO BANDS: Carved stonework from Tamerlane's tomb, Gur Emir, Samarkand. THE OTHERS: Carved marble plaques from the Necropolis of Shakhi-Zinda, Samarkand.

46

Designs from decorative painting on Bukhara architecture.

Marble prayer niche in the Tillah-Kari Medresseh and Mosque, Samarkand, 1647.

Tile decoration from the mausoleum of Kussam-ibn-Abbas in the Necropolis of
Shakhi-Zinda, Samarkand (early 14th century?).

50   Tile decoration from the mausoleum of Kussam-Ibn-Abbas, Samarkand.

Tile decoration from the Tillah-Kari Medresseh and Mosque, Samarkand.

Tile decoration from the Tillah-Kari Medresseh and Mosque, Samarkand.

Tile decoration from the Tillah-Kari Medresseh and Mosque, Samarkand.

Tilework from a mausoleum in the Necropolis of Shakhi-Zinda, Samarkand.

Tilework from a mausoleum in the Necropolis of Shakhi-Zinda, Samarkand.

Tilework from a mausoleum in the Necropolis of Shakhi-Zinda, Samarkand.

Tilework from a mausoleum in the Necropolis of Shakhi-Zinda, Samarkand.

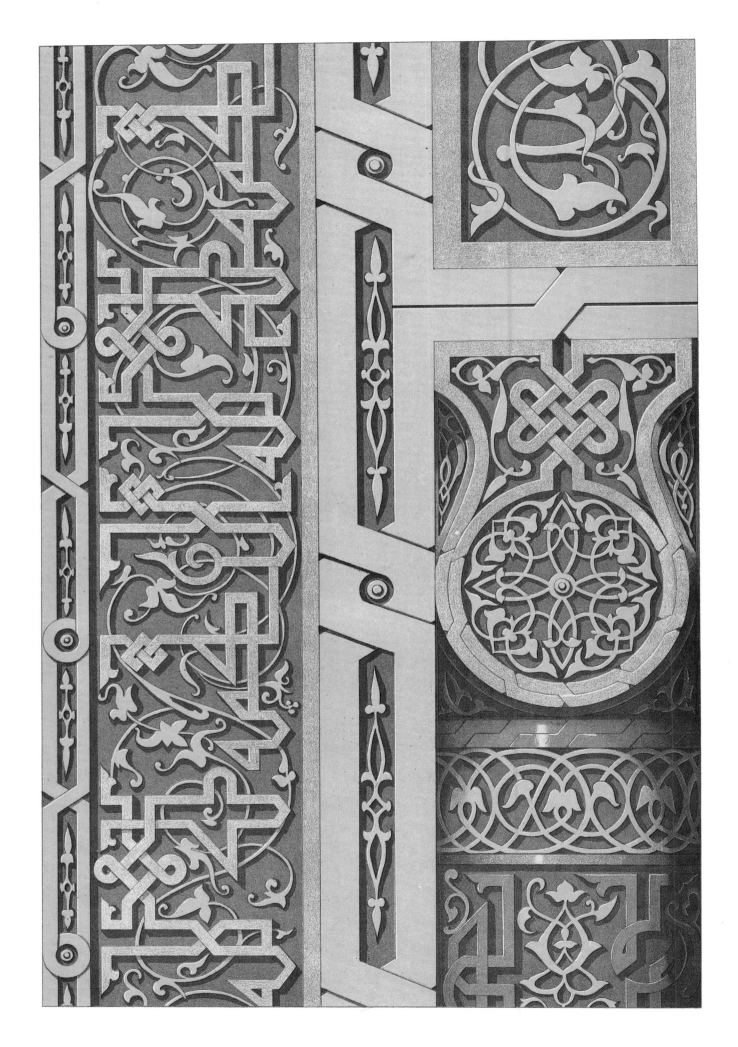

58   Architectural elements from a mausoleum in Samarkand.

Architectural elements from a mausoleum in Samarkand.

Tilework from a mausoleum in the Necropolis of Shakhi-Zinda, Samarkand.

Ceramic plates made in Tashkent.

Clay vessels made in Bukhara.

Tiles from buildings in Kunya-Urgench (not far from modern Urgench). 63

Facade of the Gur Emir, Tamerlane's mausoleum in Samarkand, begun in 1404.

Гуръ Эмиръ въ Самаркандѣ.

Могила Тимура.

Cross section of the Gur Emir.

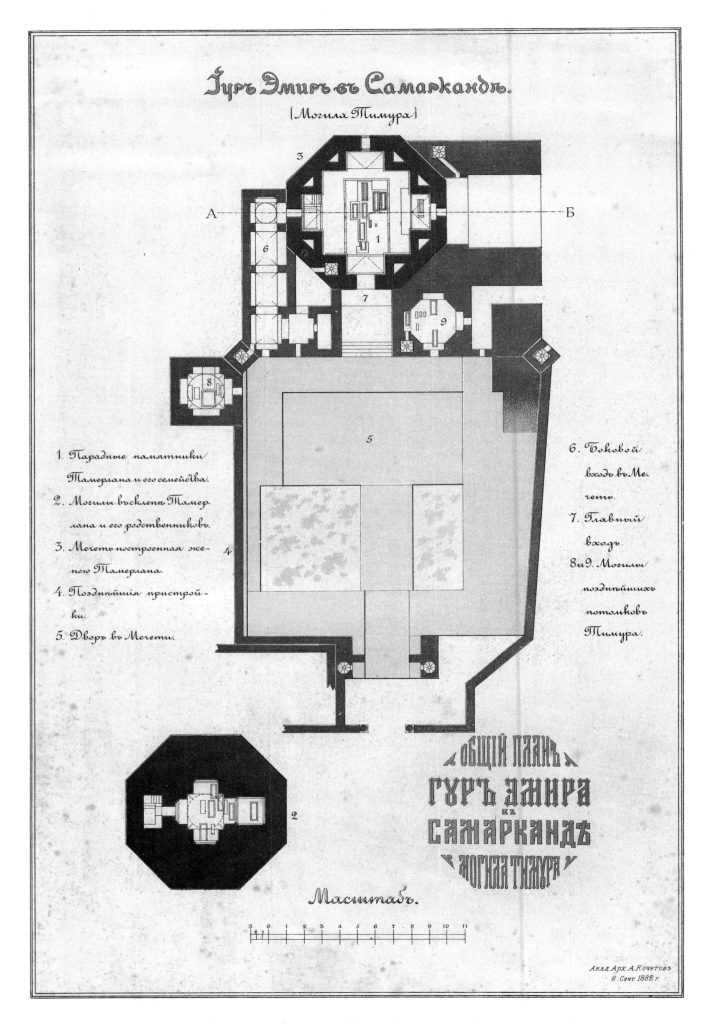

Floor plan of the Gur Emir (see Publisher's Note, page vi, for a translation of the key).

Interior of the Gur Emir with Tamerlane's Tomb.

Ruined facade of the Ak-Sarai, Tamerlane's palace in Shahr-i Sabz, begun
in 1380.